BEHIND THE SCENES BIOGRAPHIES

WHAT YOU NEVER KNEW ABOUT
RIHANNA

by Kirstie Myvett

CAPSTONE PRESS
a capstone imprint

This is an unauthorized biography.

Published by Spark, an imprint of Capstone
1710 Roe Crest Drive, North Mankato, Minnesota 56003
capstonepub.com

Copyright © 2026 by Capstone. All rights reserved. No part of this publication may be reproduced in whole or in part, or stored in a retrieval system, or transmitted in any form or by any means, electronic, mechanical, photocopying, recording, or otherwise, without written permission of the publisher.

Library of Congress Cataloging-in-Publication Data
Names: Myvett, Kirstie, author.
Title: What you never knew about Rihanna / by Kirstie Myvett.
Description: North Mankato, Minnesota : Spark, an imprint of Capstone, 2026. | Series: Behind the Scenes Biographies | Includes bibliographical references and index. | Audience: Ages 9-11 | Audience: Grades 4-6 | Summary: "Born and raised in Barbados, superstar singer Rihanna has won multiple Grammys and sold millions of records. What do her fans call themselves? What charity foundation did she start? What movies has she starred in? These questions and more will be answered in this high-interest, carefully leveled book that will enthrall reluctant and struggling readers"— Provided by publisher.
Identifiers: LCCN 2024051628 (print) | LCCN 2024051629 (ebook) | ISBN 9798875210600 (hardcover) | ISBN 9798875210556 (paperback) | ISBN 9798875210563 (pdf) | ISBN 9798875210570 (epub) | ISBN 9798875210587 (kindle edition)
Subjects: LCSH: Rihanna, 1988- —Juvenile literature. | Singers—Biography—Juvenile literature.
Classification: LCC ML3930.R44 M98 2025 (print) | LCC ML3930.R44 (ebook) | DDC 782.42164092 [B]—dc23/20241105
LC record available at https://lccn.loc.gov/2024051628
LC ebook record available at https://lccn.loc.gov/2024051629

Editorial Credits
Editor: Carrie Sheely; Designer: Elijah Blue; Media Researcher: Jo Miller; Production Specialist: Tori Abraham

Image Credits
Alamy: Cinematic, 15, Maximum Film, 14, MediaPunch Inc, 17 (left), WENN Rights Ltd, 21; Getty Images: Brad Barket, 24, 29, Frazer Harrison, cover, Icon Sportswire, 12, Jon Kopaloff, 9 (top), Kevin Mazur, 20, Kevin Winter, 4, 7, RANDY BROOKS, 11, Taylor Hill, 27, VALERIE MACON, 13; Newscom: Domine Jerome/ABACA, 23; Shutterstock: ahmadwil, 17 (makeup), Everett Collection, 18, Fahmidesign, 22 (sun), Fourdoty, 25, Nadiia Lapshynska, 26, Nganhaycuoi, 7 (heart), Nicola Pulham, 9 (bottom), Sky Cinema, 19, Sorbis, 17 (bottom right), Viktorija Reuta, 7 (shark fin), White Space Illustrations, 22 (pool)

Design Elements: Shutterstock: IIIerlok_xolms, KY726871

Any additional websites and resources referenced in this book are not maintained, authorized, or sponsored by Capstone. All product and company names are trademarks™ or registered® trademarks of their respective holders.

Printed and bound in China. 006276

TABLE OF CONTENTS

An International Superstar 4

Show What You Know, Navy Members! 6

Bajan Pride 8

Rihanna's Reign 12

The Fenty Empire 16

Bold Style 18

Rihanna's Crew 20

A Fan of Her Fans 24

A Giving Nature 26

    Glossary 30

    Read More 31

    Internet Sites 31

    Index 32

    About the Author 32

Words in **bold** are in the glossary.

AN INTERNATIONAL SUPERSTAR

Rihanna's music is loved by fans worldwide. She released her first record when she was 17 years old. She sings different kinds of music. Pop. Hip-hop. **Reggae**. **R&B**. Rihanna has done them all!

Fans call her RiRi. But did you know Rihanna is her middle name? Yes! To family and friends, she's simply Robyn.

What else is there to know about Rihanna? Let's find out!

> **FACT**
> *Rihanna* means "basil" or "sweet scent" in Arabic.

SHOW
WHAT YOU KNOW, NAVY MEMBERS!

Rihanna's top fans call themselves the Navy. Are you a member? Test your knowledge!

1. What strange place did Rihanna have a photo shoot?

2. Who is Rihanna's favorite designer?

3. Where did Rihanna find her Pomeranian Pepe?

4. What is Rihanna's favorite restaurant?

5. What is Rihanna's favorite color?

1. In a shark tank **2.** Jawara Alleyne **3.** A nightclub bathroom
4. Giorgio Baldi **5.** Lime green

BAJAN PRIDE

Robyn Rihanna Fenty was born on February 20, 1988, in St. Michael, Barbados. She lived with her parents and younger brothers, Rorrey and Rajad Fenty.

Rihanna's childhood wasn't easy. Her father struggled with drug use. Her parents divorced when she was a teen. Rihanna's mother, Monica Braithwaite, worked to support her family.

Rihanna with her mother

Rihanna's childhood home

FACT
Rihanna has two half sisters and one half brother on her father's side.

Rihanna has stayed true to her roots. She is a proud **Bajan**. Rihanna is the island's most famous citizen. In 2021, officials of Barbados named her a national hero. She enjoys spending time in her home country. She owns a **condominium** on the beach in Barbados.

"I grew up in paradise."
—Rihanna, *Vogue* interview, 2018

FACT
In 2017, the street where Rihanna lived was renamed Rihanna Drive.

Rihanna spoke after being named a Barbados national hero in 2021.

RIHANNA'S REIGN

Rihanna has won nine Grammys. She has sold more than 250 million records worldwide. Her songs and videos have more than 12 billion **streams**. She reigns as the most streamed Black woman artist on all streaming services.

FACT
In 2023, Rihanna's Superbowl LVII performance had more than 121 million viewers.

Rihanna with a Grammy award in 2008

Singing isn't Rihanna's only talent. She's also an actress. *Battleship* was her first movie. She played a Navy officer. Rihanna was a huge fan of the hit TV show, *Bates Motel*. She appeared in an episode. In 2023, she was cast to voice Smurfette in a Smurfs movie.

Rihanna in *Battleship*

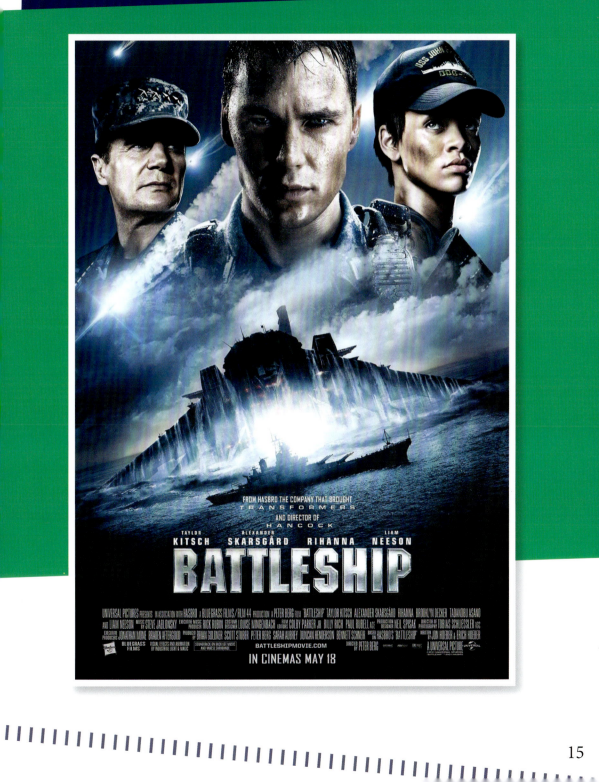

THE FENTY EMPIRE

When Rihanna was young, she loved watching her mom put on makeup. She wanted to wear makeup too.

In 2017, Rihanna started Fenty Beauty. She wanted her products to be **inclusive**. Her makeup line is for all skin shades. Fenty's success helped make Rihanna the youngest self-made American billionaire.

BOLD STYLE

Rihanna is a style **icon**. She is unafraid to try new looks. Rihanna has worn her hair long, short, blonde, black, and bright red. Her ever-changing style inspires designers and fans.

Rihanna at a benefit in New York in 2009

Rihanna at the 2015 Met Gala

At the 2015 Met Gala, Rihanna turned heads. Her yellow cape dress weighed 55 pounds (25 kilograms)! It took almost two years to make.

RIHANNA'S CREW

Rihanna has a tight circle of friends. Melissa Forde and Sonita Alexander are friends she's had since her childhood. Jennifer Rosales is also a close friend. She worked as Rihanna's assistant.

Jennifer Rosales, Rihanna, and Elena Rosales (left to right)

Melissa Forde and Rihanna

"When you find people who are great and loyal, you don't want to let go of that."
—Rihanna, *British Vogue*, 2018

In 2020, Rihanna found love with rapper A$AP Rocky. Rihanna always dreamed of becoming a mother. In 2022, her dream came true. Rihanna and A$AP had their first son, RZA.

Rihanna has many homes for her family. Her Beverly Hills house has five bedrooms, a spa, and a swimming pool.

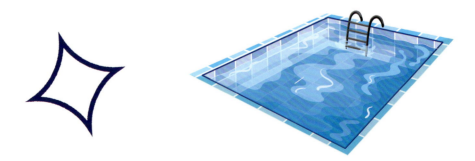

Rihanna and A$AP Rocky

FACT
A$AP's name is Rakim. Rihanna continued the tradition of *R* names with their sons RZA and Riot Rose.

A FAN
OF HER FANS

Rihanna and the Navy are tight! She takes time to meet fans and sign autographs for them. Rihanna has done fans' makeup with her beauty products.

She even featured some of her fans in her "Goodnight Gotham" music video. In it, she runs into the crowd and is held on top of their shoulders!

A GIVING NATURE

Rihanna believes in helping people. In 2012, she started the Clara Lionel Foundation (CLF). It helps people prepare for natural disasters in the Caribbean. It also helps fight climate change there and in other places. CLF is named after Rihanna's grandparents, Clara and Lionel Braithwaite.

Rihanna's **generosity** has helped many people. She partnered with an organization to improve children's education. She has done performances to support **charities**. Rihanna's light continues to shine bright like a diamond.

"... there's nothing more important than saving lives, helping lives and making lives better. This is the most important thing that I do in my life."
—Rihanna, *E! News* interview at Diamond Ball, 2019

Rihanna with children at a charity event

Glossary

Bajan (BAY-juhn)—a native of Barbados

charity (CHAYR-uh-tee)—a group that raises money or collects goods to help people in need

condominium (KON-doe-min-ee-uhm)—one unit in a building that has other units that are owned individually

generosity (je-nuh-RAH-suh-tee)—being giving

icon (EYE-kohn)—a person widely admired for having great influence in a certain area

inclusive (in-KLU-siv)—having as a goal to include everyone

R&B (ARE and BEE)—stands for rhythm and blues; R&B music developed in Black communities in the 1940s and has a soulful, emotional vocal style

reggae (RE-gay)—music from Jamaica that combines native style with rock and soul music

stream (STREEM)—to send or receive data such as music and videos over the internet

Read More

Rector, Rebecca Kraft. *Rihanna.* Mendota Heights, MN: North Star Editions, 2024.

Schwartz, Heather E. *Rihanna: Multi-Industry Mogul.* Minneapolis: Lerner Publications, 2024.

Scirri, Kaitlin. *The Business of Being a Music Influencer.* North Mankato, MN: Capstone, 2021.

Internet Sites

Biography: Rihanna
biography.com/musicians/rihanna

The Immigrant Learning Center: Robyn Rihanna Fenty
ilctr.org/about-immigrants/immigrant-entrepreneurs/hall-of-fame/robyn-rihanna-fenty

Kiddle: Rihanna Facts for Kids
kids.kiddle.co/Rihanna

Index

acting, 14
A$AP Rocky, 22, 23

Barbados, 8, 10, 11

childhood, 8
Clara Lionel Foundation (CLF), 26

fans, 5, 6, 18, 25
Fenty Beauty, 16
friends, 20

Grammys, 12, 13

helping people, 26, 28
homes, 10, 22

streams, 12
style, 18–19

videos, 12, 25

About the Author

Kirstie Myvett lives in the rich cultural and musical city of New Orleans. She enjoys foreign films, visits to the beach, and playing board games. Kirstie believes that representation matters in all places and spaces, especially in the pages of books.